VISUAL EXPLORER GUIDE
CALIFORNIA

VISUAL EXPLORER GUIDE
CALIFORNIA

SALLY COLLINGS

amber
BOOKS

First published in 2022

Published by
Amber Books Ltd
United House
North Road
London
N7 9DP
United Kingdom
www.amberbooks.co.uk
Instagram: amberbooksltd
Facebook: amberbooks
Twitter: @amberbooks
Pinterest: amberbooksltd

Project Editor: Michael Spilling
Designer: Mark Batley
Picture Research: Terry Forshaw

ISBN: 978-1-83886-202-2

Printed in China

Contents

Introduction

Gold is the defining characteristic of California in so many ways. With its hot summers and mild winters, the state sees golden sunshine most of the year. Then there is the abundance of natural resources: for millennia, Native American tribes hunted, fished and thrived among the lakes, rivers, forests, plains and mountains here. In 1848, the discovery of gold and other minerals spurred an influx of settlers to the West Coast.

Today, California is the wealthiest state in the nation, though some say its true riches lie in its winding coastline, agricultural abundance and cultural diversity. For visitors, all of these features make it the ideal place for a road trip. From the vast forests of Sequoia National Park to the rock formations of Yosemite; from the snowy peaks of the Sierra Nevada to the sun-drenched beaches in the south; from the dramatic coastal landscapes of Big Sur to the vibrant cities of Los Angeles and San Francisco, California has something for everyone.

ABOVE:
White wine grapes ready for harvest, Sonoma County.

OPPOSITE:
Streetcars have been in operation in San Francisco since 1878.

Southern California

Southern California (informally known as SoCal) is a region with two faces. The public face is movie studios, sun-soaked beaches and traffic jams. Less well-known are its fields of produce, rolling hills and snow-capped mountains. Juan Rodriguez Cabrillo was the first European to set foot on the West Coast of what is now the United States, stepping onto San Diego's shores in 1542. Nearly five centuries later, San Diego has 1.3 million inhabitants, while Los Angeles is the USA's second biggest city, with 3.8 million inhabitants. Los Angeles' Hollywood district has become synonymous with the motion picture industry and Southern California is a hub for America's television and music industries. Major entertainment companies including The Walt Disney Company, Universal, MGM, Warner Brothers and Sony are headquartered here. Southern California is also flavoured by its homegrown surf and skateboard culture. Some of the world's renowned surf spots are here: Malibu, Huntington Beach, and Santa Barbara's Rincon. The region's sunny weather and dramatic Pacific coastline are a magnet for visitors, and heavy rain is relatively unusual. In fact, earthquakes are more common: each year, Southern California has about 10,000 earthquakes, though most are so small they are not felt.

OPPOSITE:
Hollywood
Rising high above the dense-packed sprawl of Los Angeles, the Hollywood sign has become a universal metaphor for glamour and fame.

Santa Monica

Santa Monica's beach lines the coast for 5.6km (3.5 miles). It is punctuated by the lifeguard towers that resemble rustic beach huts. On the Santa Monica pier, the solar-powered Ferris wheel offers incomparable views across the ocean and inland.

LEFT:
Venice Beach
Constructed in 2009, Venice Skate Park mimics the empty swimming pools where many local skateboarders first honed their skills.

ABOVE:
Manhattan Beach
Since 1962, Manhattan Beach has hosted the annual International Surf Festival, attracting participants from all over the world. It is also a popular spot for surfers of all skill levels, its consistent surf and more than 300 days of sun per year offering year-round appeal.

Rodeo Drive

Lined with mansions and palm trees, Rodeo Drive is a 3km (2-mile) stretch of retail paradise. In 1967, the street's first high-end boutique opened: Giorgio Beverley Hills.

LA International Airport

Los Angeles International Airport (LAX) is the fourth-busiest airport in the world and the second-busiest in the United States. In 2018, 78.5 million passengers used LAX, and more than 2.4 million tons of freight and mail were processed. Its Theme Building is a prime example of the mid-century architecture style known as 'Googie'.

Dodger Stadium

Since opening its doors in 1962, Dodger Stadium has hosted more than 147 million fans. It occupies a picturesque setting, nestled in the hillside of Chavez Ravine, overlooking the San Gabriel Mountains and downtown LA.

OPPOSITE:
LA Skyline
Although it is known for its hot summers and year-long sunshine, Los Angeles is only a short drive from the San Gabriel Mountains and the Santa Monica Mountains. During winter, snow often caps the peaks.

LEFT:
Griffith Observatory
Located on the south slope of Mount Hollywood in Griffith Park, Griffith Observatory offers a view of the universe – as well as the surrounding Los Angeles basin.

Malibu

Less than 40km (25 miles) from Los Angeles, Malibu has been the destination of choice for Hollywood celebrities since the 1930s. Properties located directly on the coast or with private access to the beach can reach prices of over $100 million, making it some of the most expensive real estate in California. One of its prettiest beaches is El Matador State Beach, a secluded cove with distinctive sandstone rock towers and sea caves.

Huntington Beach

There can be few better spots to watch the sun set over the ocean than Huntington Beach Pier. It is one of the longest piers on the West Coast and rarely crowded. The pier was rebuilt after two storms in the 1980s. Now it is a great spot to watch surfers catching a wave.

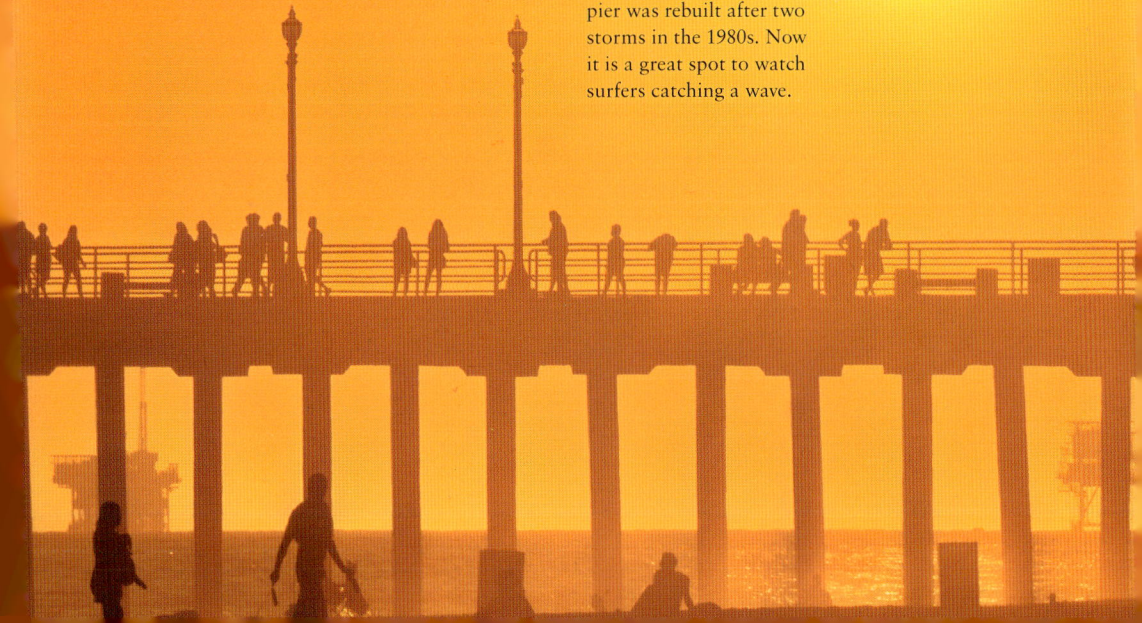

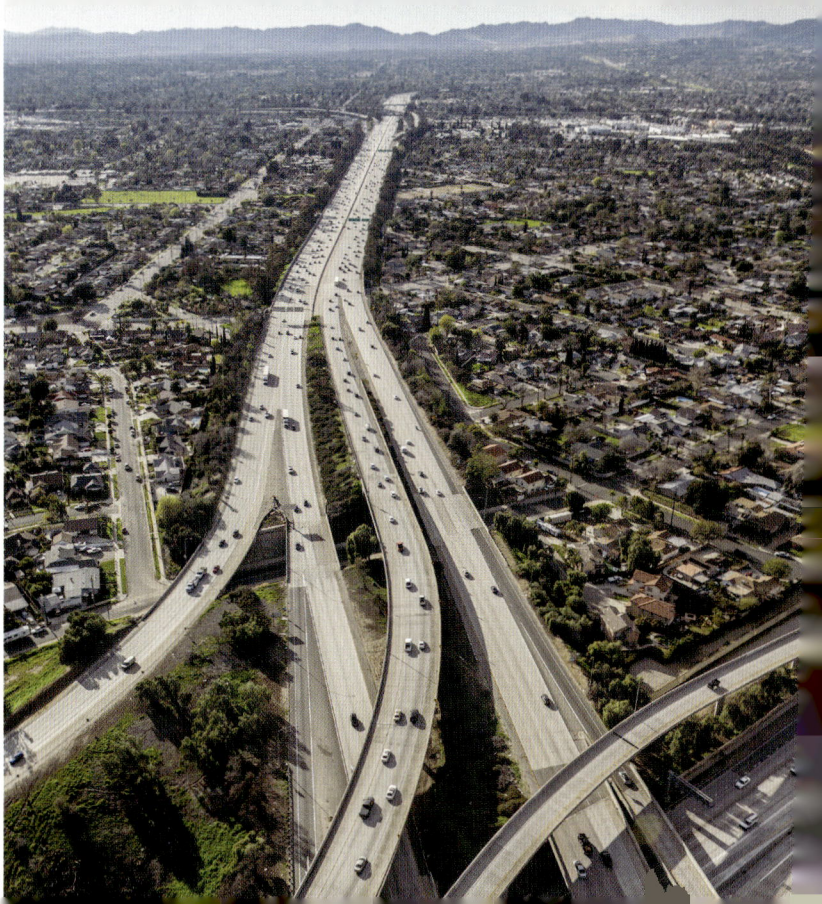

RIGHT:

San Fernando Valley
Known locally as 'The Valley', San Fernando Valley lies northwest of downtown Los Angeles. It is densely populated, ethnically diverse, studded with countless shopping malls, and home to some of the world's major movie studios.

OPPOSITE:

Anaheim
The Anaheim Regional Transportation Intermodal Center (ARTIC) features a 6,225 sq m (67,000 sq ft) interior enclosed by a network of steel tubes arching high overhead, covered with a skin of translucent pillows.

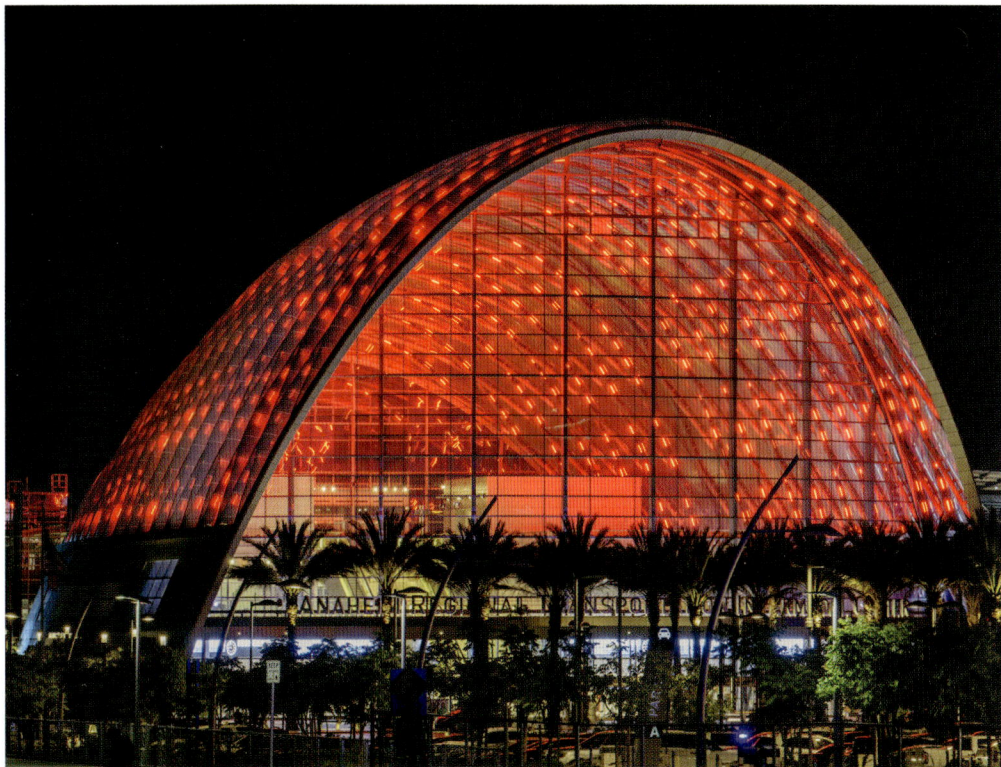

Disneyland Resort

Walt Disney's very first theme park opened its doors in Anaheim in 1955. The resort comprises Disneyland Park and Disney California Adventure Park, alongside hotels, shops and restaurants.

OPPOSITE:
Cast members
Disneyland employees
are called cast members
(or CMs). Character
performers appear before
thousands of guests each
day, posing for pictures
and creating magical
moments for adults and
children alike.

RIGHT:
Disneyland Park
Riding on Big Thunder
Mountain offers all the
thrills of a runaway
mine train. The open-
topped carriages swoop
past canyons and
through an abandoned
mine complex at nearly
50km/h (30mph).

Pasadena City Hall

Pasadena is filled with architectural gems, with examples from Art Deco, Moderne, Spanish Colonial Revival and Beaux Arts styles. In downtown Pasadena, City Hall is an example of the 'City Beautiful' movement of the early 20th century. The building's Italian Baroque dome was inspired by Venice's Santa Maria della Salute.

PASADENA
PLAYHOUSE
STATE
THEATRE
OF
CALIFORNIA
FOUNDED 1917

Pasadena Playhouse

The Pasadena Playhouse
was founded in 1917.
Its acting school trained
notable talents such as
Gene Hackman, Nick
Nolte, Dustin Hoffman
and Sally Struthers.

Rose Bowl

Pasadena's Rose Bowl
is one of the oldest
stadiums in the nation.
Built in 1921, today it
has a seating capacity
for over 92,000 people.
It has hosted five Super
Bowls, men and women's
FIFA World Cup Finals,
gold medal matches for
two Summer Olympics,
superstar concerts, and
the annual Rose Bowl
football game after which
it is named.

Surfing San Diego
Some of California's best surfing breaks await surfers in San Diego. Acclaimed surfers such as Rob Machado, Skip Frye, Debbie Beacham and Taylor Knox call San Diego home.

LEFT:
Farmers' markets
San Diego County has 54 certified farmers markets. The Little Italy Mercato is the county's largest, filling six city blocks. Here, shoppers can get to know local producers and buy direct from farmers, food makers and crafters to support the local economy.

OPPOSITE:
San Diego craft beer
San Diego boasts more than 150 independent craft breweries. The focus of the craft brewing industry is quality and customisation rather than large-scale production.

Honey Nut Pecker

IPA 7.9%

Beaker's Batch IPA 6.0

7.5	

MAIBOCK 7.0

Hibiscus IPA 6.7

American Style Light Lager 3.7

Dublin Down 4.8

7.0

Wally's Wheat Market IPA 4.8%

Belgian Style Ale Ale— 6

Berry the Hatchet 4.6

100% Kazbek hops 6.5

435 Pale Ale 5.3

Ale 4.8

LEFT:
Channel Islands
California sea lions, northern fur seals, harbour seals and northern elephant seals can all be seen on San Miguel Island, the westernmost of California's Channel Islands. Thousands breed, pup and forage on the islands' 43km (27 miles) of windswept coastline.

ABOVE AND OVERLEAF:
La Jolla
December and January are two of the best months to watch the sunset in La Jolla. Coast Boulevard also offers views of La Jolla's resident population of seals and sea lions.

LEFT:

Balboa Park

Balboa Park is the heart of San Diego. Its 485 hectares (1,200 acres) encompass 17 museums, multiple performing arts venues, gardens, trails, and other creative and recreational attractions, including the San Diego Zoo.

RIGHT:

Del Mar Beach

The Beach Boys sang about it in their 1963 song 'Surfin' USA', and Del Mar Beach is just as popular with surfers today. Lying just north of La Jolla, Del Mar also attracts sunbathers, volleyball players and families to its sandy beaches and village.

Old Town, San Diego
The first European settlement in California was built at Old Town, San Diego. Today, shops and carts in the historic marketplace offer handmade works from local and indigenous craftspeople.

LEFT:
Coronado Bridge
The landmark Coronado Bridge crosses San Diego in a sweeping arc, joining San Diego with the island of Coronado. Spanning 3.4km (2 miles), the bridge has a vertical clearance of about 61m (200ft).

Central Coast

California's Central Coast is a stretch of serenity between the high-tech hustle of the San Francisco Bay Area and the hectic energy of Southern California's cities. More than 10,000 years ago, the area was first inhabited by Chumash and other Native American people. Spanish missionaries and troops arrived in the 1770s, creating missions and small towns along the way. Some of California's best-preserved mission compounds are found in this region.

The Central Coast has no large cities: Salinas is one of its largest centres, with a population of 163,000. Relative to its small population, the Central Coast is well-supplied with colleges.

The University of California has campuses in Santa Barbara and Santa Cruz, California State University Monterey Bay is located on the site of a former military base, while California Polytechnic State University, in San Luis Obispo, was founded in 1901.

Agriculture and tourism are the region's best-known activities. The Salinas Valley is one of the most fertile farming regions in the United States, with an emphasis on crops such as strawberries and artichokes. Most visitors reach the Central Coast via the major traffic artery of US Highway 101, or the more scenic Highway 1, which hugs the curves of the Pacific coastline.

OPPOSITE:
Killer whale, Monterey Bay
Grey whales, killer whales, blue whales, humpback whales, minke whales and fin whales all migrate past the Monterey coastline at different times of year.

Monterey Bay
Old Fisherman's Wharf was built in 1845 to cater for passenger and freight vessels. Today, it is lined with restaurants and gift shops, and is a popular setting-out point for charter boats and whale-watching tours.

ABOVE:
Santa Cruz Boardwalk
A summertime family favourite since 1907, Santa Cruz Boardwalk is now a California Historic Landmark.

RIGHT:
Santa Cruz beaches
Surfers, tourists and butterflies are all drawn to Lighthouse Field State Beach. Monarch butterflies winter here during their annual migration south from the Rocky Mountains.

LEFT:

Jazz Alley, Santa Cruz
The mural points the way to Kuumbwa Jazz, a concert hall dedicated to sharing the legacy of jazz as an original American art form.

ABOVE:

Santa Cruz Boardwalk
The Boardwalk offers historic charm alongside stomach-flipping thrills. The Giant Dipper, a wooden roller coaster that first opened in 1924, has generated squeals and screams of delight for decades. The Sky Glider is a tamer way to take in the view of the beach and bay.

LEFT:
17-Mile Drive
One of the world's most famous scenic drives, 17-Mile Drive runs for 27km past landmarks such as Stillwater Cove, Del Monte Forest and the renowned Pebble Beach Golf Links.

OVERLEAF LEFT:
Pacific Grove
The Monterey cypress is one of the distinctive features of the Central Coast. The trunks are sculpted by the strong coastal winds.

OVERLEAF RIGHT:
Lovers' Point
Thanks to its east-facing orientation, Lovers' Point is one of the few spots on the West Coast where you can watch the sun rise over the water.

ALL PHOTOGRAPHS:

Carmel-by-the-Sea

It is easy to see why the city plan for Carmel-by-the-Sea is described as 'a village in a forest overlooking a white sand beach'. Carmel, as the town is also known, is a quaint slice of history, distinguished by cobblestone paths and Comstock cottages, with characteristic stone chimneys and pitched gable roofs. The town has long attracted artists and writers, and its past mayors include actor Clint Eastwood.

Bixby Bridge
Heading south from Carmel-by-the-Sea, Highway 1 traverses the scenic Bixby Bridge (or Bixby Creek Bridge). One of the highest single-span arch bridges in the world, it rises 80m (260ft) above the canyon formed by Bixby Creek.

OPPOSITE:
Bixby Bridge

Looking at the graceful span set into the rugged cliffs, it's easy to imagine that the construction of Bixby Bridge in 1932 was no easy feat. At the time, the road in was a narrow one-way zigzag. Using a system of platforms and slings, 45,000 sacks of concrete were hauled up the framework.

RIGHT:
McWay Falls

McWay Cove is a charming horseshoe of sand and tumbling surf. It is best known for McWay Falls – a pencil-slim waterfall that plunges 24m (80ft) from granite cliffs directly into the Pacific Ocean.

ALL PHOTOGRAPHS:

Highway 101

The classic Pacific Coast road trip inevitably includes Highway 101, the main north–south artery through California, Oregon and Washington states. Near Salinas, Highway 101 cuts a path between fields of crops. Known as the 'salad bowl of the world', the Salinas Valley is the world's largest producer of lettuce, as well as a top producer of strawberries, broccoli, wine grapes and other fresh produce.

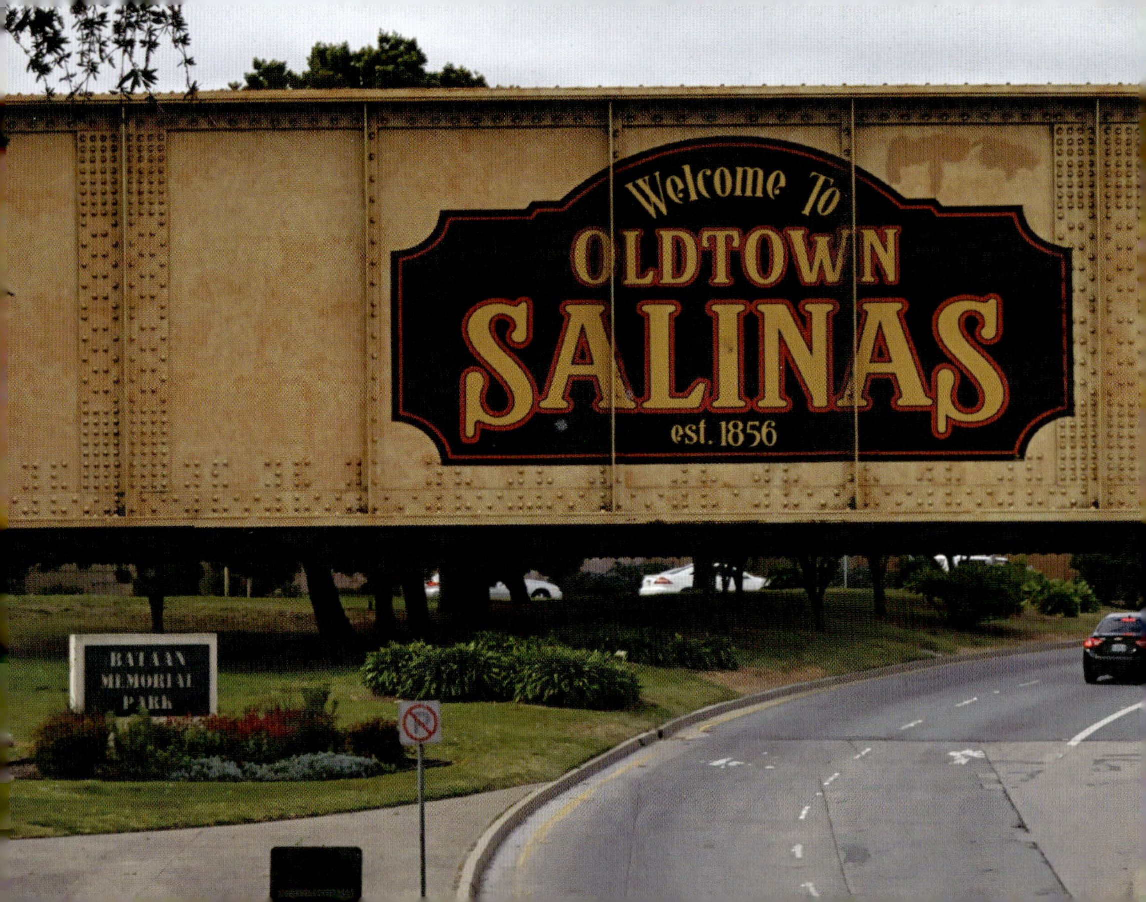
Welcome To
OLDTOWN
SALINAS
est. 1856
BATAAN
MEMORIAL
PARK

LEFT AND RIGHT:

Salinas

Salinas was the hometown of writer and Nobel laureate John Steinbeck, author of classics such as *Of Mice and Men* and *East of Eden*. Steinbeck's birthplace and childhood home, a Queen Anne-style Victorian built in 1897, has been restored and houses a restaurant and a gift store.

OVERLEAF:

Salinas Valley

A field irrigation sprinkler system waters rows of lettuce crops on farmland in the Salinas Valley. For every 0.5 hectares (1 acre) of buildings and pavement in Monterey County, there are 1.6 hectares (4 acres) of strawberries, lettuce, grapes and other crops.

15 FT

OPPOSITE:
Salinas Valley lemons
Citrus is among California's 15 top commodities and is worth $3.7 billion. That production makes California the world's biggest citrus producer.

BELOW:
Farm workers
At harvest time, the fields of Salinas Valley are packed with workers picking salad greens, strawberries and other produce. The vast majority of the 50,000 farm workers here are Latino immigrants. This is hard work – they have to wear layers of clothing to protect them from the sun, dust and bugs.

San Simeon Bay

In 1542, Portuguese navigator Rodriguez Cabrillo sailed into a small bay he named 'Bay of Sardines'. Today, we know it as San Simeon Bay. Tucked away from the traffic passing on nearby Highway 1, it is a popular spot to relax, with its emerald waters, recreational pier, and dog-friendly stretches of sand.

Elephant seals
In autumn, northern
elephant seals migrate
to California's coastline.
Adult males can grow
up to 2,000kg (2.2 tons),
around the size of an
Indian rhino.

San Simeon
Windsurfers are drawn to
spots such as San Simeon
because of the windy
conditions. Wind speeds
here have been known to
reach 64km/h (40mph).

ALL PHOTOGRAPHS:

Hearst Castle

Gaudy, glamorous, eccentric, visionary – Hearst Castle has been described in all these ways, and more. Built on a hilltop overlooking the Pacific Coast, the estate was the brainchild of newspaper tycoon William Randolph Hearst. Starting in 1919, Hearst worked with California's first licensed female architect, Julia Morgan, over 28 years to construct a castle to match Europe's finest. The result is an opulent rendition of the Mediterranean Revival style, its facade evoking a Spanish cathedral with its bell towers and ornate decorations.

Pismo Beach

A classic Californian beach town, Pismo Beach offers white sand beaches and spectacular views of the sun setting over the Pacific Ocean. Pismo State Beach is flanked by sea caves and coves, and is set against a background of dramatic bluffs. Pismo Pier has been rebuilt many times over, having been pulled apart by the wild storms that lash the coast. The current structure acts as an unofficial town square: locals and tourists alike stroll the pier, fish for red snapper and ling cod, or watch the surfers in the waves below.

LEFT:

Santa Barbara
Its blend of Spanish influence, coastal vibe and upscale shopping and dining make Santa Barbara a popular destination. Known as the 'American Riviera', the coastal town enjoys a Mediterranean climate.

RIGHT:

County produce
Agriculture is Santa Barbara County's major industry. Strawberries are the leading crop, alongside cauliflower, broccoli, flowers, wine grapes and other fruits.

LEFT:

Pelicans, Santa Barbara
The only breeding
grounds for California
brown pelicans in the
western United States are
in the Channel Islands,
just off the coast near
Santa Barbara.

OPPOSITE:

Santa Barbara Mission
Known as 'Queen of
the Missions' for its
exceptional beauty, the
Santa Barbara Mission
was founded by Spanish
Franciscans in 1786.
It is the only mission
continuously operated
by the Franciscans since
its founding.

San Francisco
& the Bay Area

San Francisco and the surrounding Bay Area has long been a magnet to those seeking riches. In 1848, it was a hub for the Gold Rush, with tens of thousands of people from all over the world travelling here to find their fortune. The history of San Francisco was also shaped by the 1950s Beat poets and the Summer of Love in the 1960s, and much of the city's modern cultural identity is built on those foundations. Today, the region still offers both cultural and monetary riches to its population of over seven million people.

Outside of San Francisco, the Bay Area is headquarters of some of the biggest technology companies in the world, including Apple and Google. A short drive from the bustling cities and technology there are beautiful redwood forests and rolling hills. Visitors can enjoy an abundance of wineries, especially in Napa and Sonoma. The area's climate is described as Mediterranean, with hot, dry summers and cool, rainy winters. Yet San Francisco is better known for its rain and fogs: its position on a peninsula surrounded by cold water gives it a climate all of its own.

OPPOSITE:
Cable cars
The cable car was invented in San Francisco in 1873. Three different cable car lines operate in San Francisco: the Powell-Mason, Powell-Hyde and California Street lines.

OPPOSITE:

Golden Gate Bridge
The Golden Gate Bridge connects the city of San Francisco to the hills of Marin County in the north. When it was built in 1937, the suspension bridge was considered an engineering marvel – at 2.7km (1.7 miles), it was the longest main suspension bridge span in the world.

ABOVE:

Fort Point
Nestled beneath the southern approach to the Golden Gate Bridge lies Fort Point, built at the height of the Gold Rush to protect San Francisco Bay from foreign attack.

Downtown San Francisco

The sun sets over Market Street, one of San Francisco's main traffic arteries. Around it, office buildings crowd, testament to San Francisco's position as tech capital of the United States. The Bay Area is widely considered the most important region in the world for new technology startups and venture capital.

ALL PHOTOGRAPHS:

Lombard Street

More like an amusement park ride than a public road, San Francisco's Lombard Street is claimed to be 'the crookedest street in the world'. It was designed this way in 1922, as a way of reducing the hill's natural 27 per cent grade, which was considered too steep for both cars and pedestrians.

LEFT:
Alamo Square
Alamo Square is one of the best places to appreciate San Francisco's Victorian architecture, including the famous Painted Ladies.

ABOVE:
Haight-Ashbury district
Made famous by the hippie movement in the 1960s, San Francisco's Haight-Ashbury neighbourhood has been home to famous singers (including the Grateful Dead and Janis Joplin) and headquarters for the Hell's Angels. A pair of legs in fishnet stockings and red heels has been hanging out of this window since the 1960s.

Alcatraz

America's most infamous prison, Alcatraz is perched on a rocky island in San Francisco Bay. The prison was abandoned in 1963 because it was too expensive to maintain: its isolation meant that food, fuel, and even fresh water had to be brought to the island by barge.

SEA LION 25th ANNIVERSARY

PIER
39

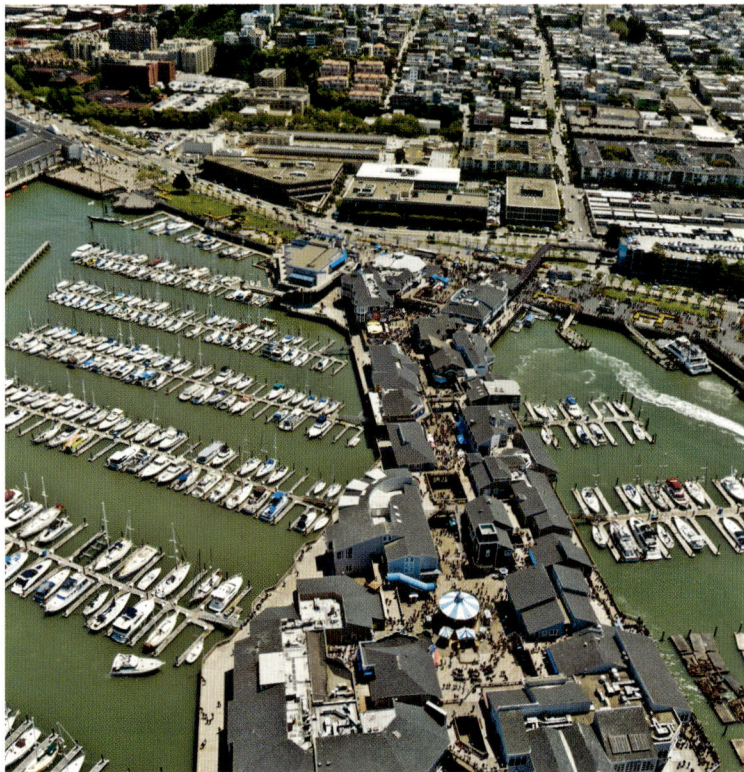

ALL PHOTOGRAPHS:

Pier 39

From late summer to late spring, hundreds of sea lions frequent Pier 39's K-Dock. They have been coming here since shortly after the Loma Prieta earthquake in 1989, when locals started moving their boats away from the pier. The appeal for them is that there's plenty of herring in San Francisco Bay, and the sea lions' natural predators (white sharks and orcas) do not typically feed there.

Chinatown
Dragon Gate on Bush
Street is the official
entrance into San
Francisco's Chinatown.
The gate is an authentic
entry gate like those seen
in Chinese towns, and
was a gift from Taiwan
in 1969. The quote in
Chinese from Dr Sun
Yat Sen (founder of the
Chinese Republic) says
'All under heaven is for
the good of the people'.

OPPOSITE:
Chinese New Year
San Francisco's
Chinatown contains
the largest Chinese
population outside of
Asia. Its Chinese New
Year Parade is one of
the few remaining night
illuminated parades
in North America and
the biggest parade
celebrating the lunar new
year outside of Asia.

Telegraph Hill

One of San Francisco's famous 'Seven Hills', Telegraph Hill is also the name of the neighbourhood surrounding it. It is perhaps best known for being the site of Coit Tower, a slender concrete column that peeks above the top of the San Francisco skyline. Its observation deck provides 360-degree views across the city to the Golden Gate and Bay bridges. A remarkable series of murals inside the tower's base, painted in 1934, depict life in California during the Great Depression.

San Francisco–Oakland Bay Bridge

Within its 1165 sq km (450 square miles) of landlocked harbour, San Francisco Bay has eight major highway bridges, including the Bay Bridge (as locals call it). It is the longest steel high-level bridge in the world, and almost a quarter of a million vehicles cross it every day. At night, its elegant span is illuminated by 48,000 LED lights suspended from 1,521 light fixtures.

Silicon Valley

South of San Francisco lies Silicon Valley, named for the primary material found in computer microprocessors. It is most famous for being the world's first 'high-technology region', and even today continues to foster thousands of tech startups. The region is home to some of the world's richest people, as well as one of the world's hottest real estate markets. The valley itself is flanked by the Diablo Range to the east and the Santa Cruz Mountains to the west.

Apple Park Visitor Center
Opened in 2017,
Apple's new corporate
headquarters in
Cupertino is a ring-
shaped building, entirely
powered by renewable
energy, and features the
world's largest panels of
curved glass.

eBay HQ
eBay operates the
world's largest online
auction sites from its
headquarters in San Jose,
at the southernmost part
of Silicon Valley.

LEFT:
Tiburon
A short ferry ride from San Francisco lies Tiburon, a quaint town packed with shops and restaurants – and visitors on sunny weekends. The town's name was taken from the Spanish word *tiburón*, meaning 'shark'.

ABOVE:
Sausalito
The colourful houseboats of Sausalito have become the bayside town's best-known feature over the past few decades. In the 1960s, the abandoned boat slips here were colonized by artists, writers, musicians and bohemians.

Muir Woods

Visitors come to marvel at the old-growth redwood trees of Muir Woods, which was declared a National Monument in 1908. The trees range in age from 400 to 800 years, and reach heights up to 76m (250ft). Wildlife in the forest include woodpeckers, owls, deer, chipmunks, skunks and squirrels.

Mt Tamalpais peak
The 784m (2,571ft) peak of Mt Tamalpais offers a panoramic view of San Francisco Bay and the Pacific Ocean. In 1770, two explorers named the mountain La Sierra de Nuestro Padre de San Francisco, but that name was later changed to the Miwok word, Tamalpais.

Mt Tamalpais
Because of its height and
proximity to the coast,
Mt Tamalpais creates
its own microclimate,
condensing the coastal
fog to hydrate the
redwoods and hills.

ALL PHOTOGRAPHS
AND OVERLEAF:

Stinson Beach

North of San Francisco across the Golden Gate Bridge lies Stinson Beach. The beach backs up to Bolina Lagoon, where great egrets and great blue herons nest each spring. On a sunny day the white-sand beach attracts swimmers, surfers and para-surfers. Hikers and mountain bikers also come here to access a vast network of trails leading from the coast to Muir Woods and Mt Tamalpais.

Sonoma County

At the northern edge of the San Francisco Bay Area lies Sonoma County, a laid-back region with a global reputation for winemaking. The diverse terrain and microclimates make it possible to grow a wide array of grape varieties, including chardonnay, cabernet sauvignon, pinot noir, merlot and zinfandel.

ALL PHOTOGRAPHS:

Napa Valley
Perhaps the most celebrated winegrowing region in the US, Napa Valley is surprisingly one of the smallest. Less than four per cent of all US wine comes from the region, but its beauty and proximity to San Francisco make it a magnet for tourists and wine lovers.

Northern California

Although it is home to Sacramento, California's capital city, there aren't many urban centres in Northern California – and the further north you travel, the fewer cities you will find. Instead, the region (commonly known as NorCal) is distinguished by sweeping forests and a largely farm-based economy. The first influx of settlers was prompted by California's Gold Rush, which began when gold was discovered at Sutter's Mill in Coloma on 24 January 1848. In the deacdes that followed Northern California was transformed, its population swelling and its economy thriving.

As the gold boom subsided, farming became the main economic driver. Particularly in the Sacramento Valley, much of the land has been farmed by the same families for many generations. Today, rice, nuts, fruit, tomatoes and wine propel its economy. Most visitors to Northern California follow the coast. Known as the Redwood Coast, it stretches north to the Oregon border. The dense redwood forests continue inland among rugged mountains carved by river valleys and canyons. The coastal lands are often layered in fog, while inland the baking sunshine of summer gives way to blankets of snow in winter.

OPPOSITE:
Avenue of the Giants
Sunrays fall on ancient giant redwoods along the Avenue of the Giants. This famous scenic drive is part of the original Highway 101.

Battery Point Lighthouse
Perched on top of a small
rocky island just off the
shore near Crescent City,
Battery Point was one
of the West Coast's first
lighthouses. It was built
in the favoured style of
a central brick tower
protruding from the
roof of a Cape Cod-style
stone house. Visitors can
only reach it by foot at
low tide.

ALL PHOTOGRAPHS:
Crescent City
Located just south of the Oregon border, Crescent City is both the gateway to the redwood forests and an active fishing harbour. Once home to the Tolowa and Yurok peoples, Crescent City became a hub for the gold-mining, whaling and timber industries in the mid-1800s. The surrounding waters offer some of the West Coast's most productive fishing grounds for salmon, groundfish, crab and shrimp.

Eureka

The California Gold Rush brought settlers to Humboldt Bay in the 1850s. Its main city is named Eureka from the Greek word meaning 'I have found it'. Many of the ornate Victorian buildings sprung up during the ensuring lumber boom, an era of settler prosperity.

RIGHT:

The Pink Lady

One of Eureka's fine examples of Queen Anne architecture is the Pink Lady. Built in 1889, it features highly ornamental exterior wall surfaces, including scalloped shingles.

Noyo Harbor

Just south of Fort Bragg, Noyo Harbor is a working port with a marina. It is a setting-out point for whale-watching and crab-catching cruises, and ocean-fishing charters. From June to September, salmon, ling cod, snapper and albacore tuna can be caught in these waters.

OPPOSITE:

Highway 1

A classic California road trip follows Highway 1 along the coastal contours of Mendocino County, winding through 'tree tunnels' along the way.

RIGHT:

Glass Beach

Smooth 'sea glass' abounds among the pebbles at Glass Beach on the Mendocino Coast. Shards of broken bottles, windows and other glass debris have been worn down over decades by the ocean waves, leaving behind smooth gem-like pieces in many colours.

ALL PHOTOGRAPHS:

Mendocino Lighthouses
The rocky Mendocino Coast has long been guarded by a string of lighthouses. Point Arena Lighthouse is surrounded by water on three sides, offering majestic views of the Pacific Ocean. The Cape Mendocino lighthouse (opposite) was installed at the westernmost point in the state of California. After years of taking a beating from weather and earthquakes, it was moved 48km (30 miles) south, to Shelter Cove.

Sundial Bridge

Designed by Spanish architect Santiago Calatrava, the Sundial Bridge spans the Sacramento River in Redding. Its glass block walkway, white tower and suspension cables form a working sundial, one of the world's largest. The bridge was constructed without supports in the river bed to avoid disturbing the salmon-spawning habitat below.

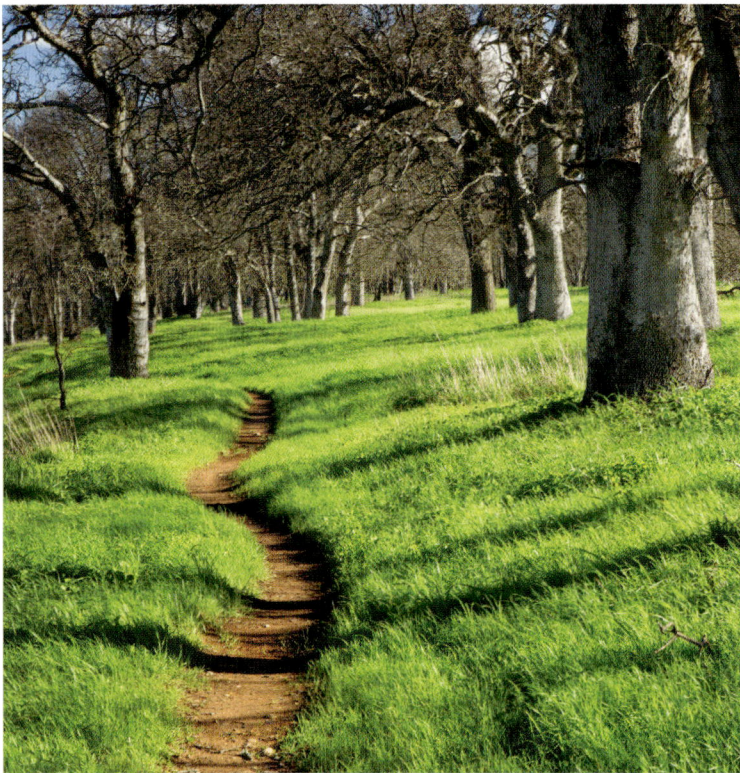

LEFT:

Sacramento River Trail

The Sacramento River Bend Area of Critical Environmental Concern lies along California's largest river. Its wildlife includes bald eagles, osprey, deer and salmon.

OPPOSITE:

Redding

Redding is known for its sunshine, hiking trails and fishing. Just upstream of the city, Keswick Dam marks the end of the free-flowing reach of the Sacramento River. It is the highest point upstream at which salmon and steelhead spawn.

ALL PHOTOGRAPHS:

Sacramento
Lying at the confluence of the Sacramento and American Rivers, the city of Sacramento is the state capital of California. With the California Gold Rush, Sacramento became a major commercial centre, serving as the terminus for the Pony Express and the First Transcontinental Railroad. Now, the state government is the city's largest employer.

Tower Bridge

Constructed in 1935, Sacramento's Tower Bridge is a vertical lift bridge, allowing large boats to pass below. Its golden colour was chosen to symbolise the California Gold Rush that fuelled the city's economic development.

OPPOSITE:

Orange groves

The San Joaquin Valley lies south of the Sacramento–San Joaquin River Delta. Predominantly rural, it is the heart of California's citrus belt.

ABOVE:

Shasta Lake

In a quiet corner of northern California, Shasta Lake is the largest reservoir in California. Water skiing, houseboating and fishing are popular. Above it rises the perpetually snowcapped Mount Shasta.

PREVIOUS PAGES:

Auburn, Placer County
Gold rush history
lives on in towns like
Auburn, where Old West
architecture has been
preserved and a statue of
gold prospector Claude
Chana marks the entrance
to the Old Town. Today,
visitors are drawn year-
round to Auburn for
its restaurants, antique
stores and street fairs.

RIGHT:

Vineyards
More than 60 per cent
of the wine produced in
California comes from
grapes grown in the San
Joaquin Valley. The first
grapes were planted in
the 1850s to quench the
thirst of the gold-seekers
flooding in to California.

Mountains, Forests & National Parks

Beyond California's famous beaches and cities lie natural treasures of many kinds. The state contains 7,971 named mountains, with Mount Whitney crowned as tallest at 4,421m (14,505ft). Lake Tahoe is the epicentre of California's ski slopes, with fine powder and 300 days of sunshine each year. Nearly every section of the state offers forests to explore, from redwood forests in the north to chaparral and pine groves in the south. Although 40 per cent of California's forestland is owned by families, Native American tribes or private companies, 18 national forests have been established to protect California's wilderness. California also boasts nine national parks, more than any other state. Each has its own unique appeal. For big trees, Kings Canyon and Sequoia are both outstanding. To escape civilisation, head to the Channel Islands. Yosemite National Park is a World Heritage site and it's easy to see why. And with 7,240km (4,500 miles) of trails, even the state's most secluded landscapes can be accessed by nature lovers.

OPPOSITE:
Yosemite National Park
The granite slopes around Olmsted Point are strewn with giant boulders left behind by the most recent glacial period, around 20,000 years ago.

ALL PHOTOGRAPHS:

Six Rivers National Forest

Encompassing six rivers, four counties and over 400,000 hectares (one million acres) of land, Six Rivers National Forest is best known for its pristine woodlands. The forest's ecosystems provide habitat for several threatened and endangered species, including the bald eagle and the peregrine falcon. Wildflowers such as the western azalea add a delicate touch to the landscape.

Salmon River

Every spring, whitewater rafting enthusiasts flock to Salmon River in the Klamath National Forest. The snowmelt creates premier rafting conditions on this remote river that plunges through a narrow steep-walled gorge of glistening marble and granite.

Burney Falls

One of the most spectacular waterfalls in California, Burney Falls are at their most intense during spring.

Shasta-Trinity National Forest

Over 35 species of trees grow in the Shasta-Trinity National Forest, from oaks and madrone at lower elevations to aspens, pines and cedars on the higher slopes.

Stuart Fork Creek

The rivers of Shasta-Trinity National Forest offer excellent fishing and ample wildlife-viewing.

ALL PHOTOGRAPHS:
Redwood National Park
Part of a complex of several state and national parks in Northern California, Redwood National Park protects the tallest trees on the planet. Some specimens are more than 113m (370ft) high, making them five stories taller than the Statue of Liberty. The park's forests, hills, rivers and coastline are watered by moisture from both heavy winter rains and persistent summer fog.

BELOW:
Elk sparring
Two bull elks spar in Redwood National Park during the annual elk rut. In autumn, the males become aggressive and may charge at humans.

OPPOSITE:
Mendocino National Forest
The only one of California's 18 national forests that is not accessible by paved road, the Mendocino National Forest offers solitude. The region's naturally alkaline and carbonated hot springs were used by local Native Americans for thousands of years, and from the early 1900s drew western visitors.

Lassen Peak

Beyond the tranquil waters of Manzanita Lake rises Lassen Peak. Compared to the four million visitors that flock to Yosemite each year, Lassen Volcanic Park sees only 400,000 people annually. They come to see its volcanic domes, numerous hydrothermal areas, and lush mountain landscapes.

LEFT:

Plumas National Forest
Heavy tree cover adorns the slopes in Plumas National Forest, set between the Sierra Nevada and the Cascade Ranges. The area was once much used for logging, but the federal government now prohibits this in national forests.

RIGHT:

Feather Falls
A Yosemite-style waterfall without the crowds, Feather Falls displays nature's grandeur in a dramatic Sierra Nevada setting. The hike to the viewing platform takes several hours, but offers a spectacular outlook.

Lake Tahoe
The Lake Tahoe region is popular in all seasons. Summer is warm enough for beach and water activities, while winter brings more than 1,000cm (400in) of snow to Tahoe's ski resorts.

ALL PHOTOGRAPHS:

Eldorado National Forest

The miners who came to California in the gold rush of 1849 called the land El Dorado after the legendary South American 'land of gold'. Today, Eldorado National Forest's treasure lies in its rivers, lakes and streams that are alive with fish; mountains and meadows for skiing; and campsites and picnic areas in dense alpine forests.

Sequoia National Park

Giant sequoias are the largest trees on the planet, and they grow only on the western slopes of the Sierra Nevada in California. Sequoia National Park holds 40 giant sequoia groves, ranging from one to tens of thousands of sequoia trees per grove. The giant sequoias' red-orange bark stands out among the grey and brown bark of other trees.

BELOW AND OVERLEAF:

Mount Whitney
At 4,421m (14,505ft),
Mount Whitney is the
highest mountain in
the contiguous United
States. In the indigenous
Paiute language, Mount
Whitney is called
Tumanguya, meaning
'the very old man'.

Because Mount
Whitney is the most
frequently climbed
mountain peak in the
Sierra Nevada, a permit
system is in place to
restrict the number of
day-hikers. At the summit
is a small, stone hut built
in 1909.

RIGHT:

Moro Rock
Moro Rock is a dome-
shaped granite monolith
in the centre of Sequoia
National Park. The 400-
step Moro Rock Staircase
leads to spectacular
views across the Great
Western Divide.

LEFT:

Goddard Canyon
The Goddard Canyon trail climbs through lightly wooded sections and open meadows, crossing seasonal streams that flow down the steep canyon walls.

ABOVE:

Muir Hut
High on the summit of Muir Pass sits the granite structure of Muir Hut. It is a memorial to John Muir, an early wilderness advocate, as well as a functional shelter for backpackers and hikers.

El Capitan

Located on the north side of Yosemite Valley, El Capitan is one of the most recognisable rock formations in the world. Its 2,740m (3,000ft) of sheer granite is a beacon for photographers and one of the world's top challenges for climbers.

OPPOSITE:

Yosemite Falls
Glacier Point offers
a spectacular view of
Yosemite Falls, one of
the tallest waterfalls in
North America.

ABOVE:

Merced River
The cool waters of
Yosemite's Merced
River lend themselves to
swimming and tubing.
The Merced flows
through exceptional
scenery – glaciated peaks,
lakes and meadows –
in alternating pools
and cascades.

Half Dome

Named for its distinctive cut-off shape, Half Dome rises nearly 1,500m (5,000ft) above Yosemite Valley. The climb to the top is strenuous, taking most hikers 10 to 12 hours.

Tenaya Lake

One of Yosemite's largest bodies of water, Tenaya Lake is usually buried under snow through winter. On rare occasions the ice is exposed, enticing people to ice-skate and play hockey against a backdrop of granite domes and ridges.

Donnell Reservoir

In a remote gorge of the Stanislaus River Canyon lies Donnell Reservoir, one of California's prettiest lakes. It is only accessible by a 90-minute drive on rough forest roads, or by hiking an unmarked national forest trail.

Manzanita tree

Ranging from small shrubs to towering trees, manzanitas have distinctive reddish or orange bark and waxy leaves. Their apple-like fruits give the trees their name, meaning 'little apple' in Spanish.

Eastern Sierra Nevadas

The Sierra Nevada range is California's backbone, and the Eastern Sierra offers one of California's most spectacular road trips. The ideal time to make the journey is late spring or fall, when the mountains are dusted with snow but the roads remain passable.

Deserts

California's deserts are extraordinary. Cacti stretch spiny fingers towards the searing blue sky; eagles, desert tortoises, coyotes and desert bighorn sheep make their home here; bizarre sand dunes and rock formations provide an other-worldly air. By definition, a desert is any large, extremely dry area of land with sparse vegetation. The California Desert Conservation Area covers more than 10 million hectares (25 million acres), almost a quarter of the state's total land area. Concentrated in the southeast, California's desert region consists of the Mojave, Colorado and Great Basin Deserts. Each has its own characteristics, but all are hot and dry, receiving less than 25cm (10in) of rain each year. Death Valley is the driest place in North America, receiving less than 5cm (2in) of rain every year. It is also the hottest place on Earth: a world-record air temperature of 57°C (134°F) was recorded at Furnace Creek on 10 July 1913. Hostile though such an environment may seem, visitors are drawn to California's deserts to hike, camp and sightsee. Far from the big cities and with impeccably clear air, the deserts offer rainbow sunsets, star-speckled night skies, spectacular terrain, and explosions of wildflowers in early spring.

OPPOSITE:
Joshua Tree National Park
Two deserts meet in this park: the higher-elevation Mojave Desert and the lower Colorado Desert.

Joshua Tree National Park

The spiky Joshua tree is native to the arid southwestern United States, and only grows in the most adverse conditions. They thrive in the western half of Joshua Tree National Park, with its sandy soil covered by massive granite boulders and rock piles.

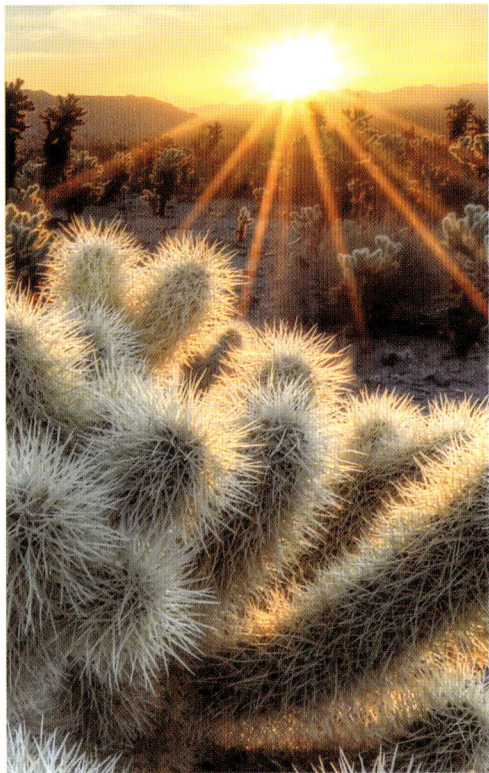

Desert Blooms
Desert globemallow
is one of the flowering
species in Joshua Tree
National Park. In wet
years it forms spectacular
displays through the
northern sections of
the park.

Jumbo Rocks
The aptly named Jumbo
Rocks campground in
Joshua Tree National
Park is set among giant
sculpted boulders.
Visitors climb the rock
formations to enjoy
impressive views.

PREVIOUS PAGES:
Route 66, Mojave Desert
No other US highway
is more fabled than
Route 66. It skirts the
Mojave Desert before
passing through Los
Angeles and ending at
the Pacific Ocean.

OPPOSITE:
Rainbow Basin
In the Mojave Desert,
rocks in shades of green,
lavender and ochre
contrast with the intense
blue desert sky.

RIGHT:
Blooming cactus
The Mojave wildflower
show doesn't occur every
year, but a few soaking
storms in winter and
early spring will produce
a memorable bloom.

LEFT:
Wildrose charcoal kilns
Ten beehive-shaped kilns are among the most remarkable historical features of Death Valley National Park. In 1875, lead ore was discovered in the region. These kilns were constructed to produce charcoal as fuel for silver-lead smelters.

BELOW:
Wild horses
Thousands of wild horses roam the deserts of California. In the blazing hot summer, the horses travel up to 8km (5 miles) to find water.

Ghost towns

California's ghost towns are a symbol of the boom and bust that defined the state. The discovery of gold and other minerals sparked a flood of people seeking their fortune. The town of Calico's rise was spurred by the discovery of silver ore in 1881. At its peak, the town had a red-light district and 22 saloons. Mining declined when the price of silver fell, and the town was nearly desolate by 1929.

Barstow

Once a bustling mining centre and railroad town, in the early 19th century Barstow was a jumping off place for immigrants entering the state on the original US Route 66, as made famous by John Steinbeck's novel, *The Grapes of Wrath*. Today the town is a favoured starting point for touring the western Mojave Desert.

ABOVE:

The Racetrack

Littered across the flat surface of the Racetrack, a 'playa' (dry lakebed) in Death Valley, are rocks that seem to have been dragged mysteriously across the ground. Some leave trails that stretch for hundreds of yards.

OPPOSITE:

Zabriskie Point

Zabriskie Point offers a panoramic view across Death Valley National Park's 'badlands'.

Salt flats

At 86m (282ft) below sea level, Badwater Basin in Death Valley is the lowest point in North America. Salt flats are too harsh for most plants and animals to survive, yet are quite fragile. The delicate crystals are easily crushed, so vehicles are not permitted to drive here.

Death Valley

Death Valley showcases the subtle beauty of desert environments. Its remarkable canyons, hills and gullys are the result of fault activity through the centuries, but also crustal sinking, volcanic activity and rapid erosion.

ALL PHOTOGRAPHS:
**Anza Borrego
Desert State Park**
Only two hours east of
San Diego's beaches,
Anza Borrego Desert
State Park is famous for
its majestic views and
natural wonders.

Visitors can discover
slot canyons and cactus-
studded hills, natural
palm oases and spring
wildflowers.

LEFT:

Metal sculptures
Around the town of Borrego Springs, more than 130 metal sculptures rise from the desert landscape. They are the creations of self-taught sculptor Ricardo Breceda.

OPPOSITE:

Bighorn sheep
Listed as a federally endangered species in 1998, desert bighorn sheep are found in several parts of Anza Borrego Desert State Park. Bighorns inhabit rugged and open habitats such as rocky slopes, cliffs and canyons.

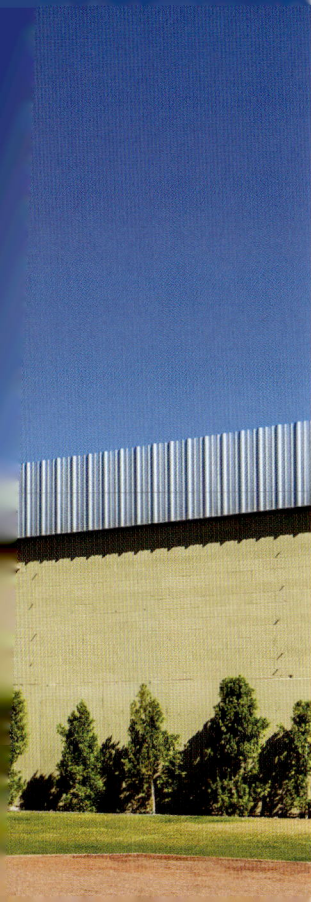

LEFT:
'Forever Marilyn'
An 8m (26ft) tall statue of Marilyn Monroe presides over Palm Springs, a popular resort city in the Sonoran Desert.

ABOVE:
Palm Springs
This upscale desert city sits at the foot of Mount San Jacinto, in an area long famous for its hot springs. Palm Springs became well-known in the 1920s when Hollywood movie stars made it their weekend retreat of choice.

Wind farm
Visitors approaching Palm Springs from the east are greeted by the sight of 4,000 wind turbines sprouting in the desert. The San Gorgonio Pass wind farm provides enough electricity to power Palm Springs and the surrounding Coachella Valley.

Picture Credits